Energy Choices

Wind Energy

Julie Richards

Marshall Cavendish
Benchmark
New York

This edition first published in 2010 in the United States of America
by Marshall Cavendish Benchmark.

Marshall Cavendish Benchmark
99 White Plains Road
Tarrytown, NY 10591
www.marshallcavendish.us

First published in 2009 by
MACMILLAN EDUCATION AUSTRALIA PTY LTD
15–19 Claremont Street, South Yarra 3141

Visit our website at www.macmillan.com.au or go directly to www.macmillanlibrary.com.au

Associated companies and representatives throughout the world.

Copyright © Julie Richards 2009

Library of Congress Cataloging-in-Publication Data

Richards, Julie.
  Wind energy / by Julie Richards.
    p. cm. – (Energy choices)
  Includes index.
  ISBN 978-0-7614-4430-5
  1. Wind power–Juvenile literature. I. Title.
  TJ820.R5 2009
  333.9'2–dc22
                                    2009005910

Text and cover design by Christine Deering
Page layout by Domenic Lauricella
Photo research by Legend Images
Illustrations by Richard Morden

Printed in the United States

Acknowledgments

The author and the publisher are grateful to the following for permission to reproduce copyright material:

Front cover photograph: Wind turbines on rolling hills, California © Terrance Emerson/iStockphoto

Photos courtesy of:
123rf/Rusty Dodson, 17 (left); © Taiga/Dreamstime.com, 22 (right); © Clearviewstock/Dreamstime.com, 19; © Manonringuette/
Dreamstime.com, 29; © Seraphic/Dreamstime.com, 12; Kazuhiro Nogi/AFP/Getty Images, 8; Sean Gallup/Getty Images, 26; ©
Ricardo De Mattos/iStockphoto, 3, 22 (left); © Terrance Emerson/iStockphoto, 1; © Izabela Habur/iStockphoto, 30 (right); © Maciej
Korzekwa/iStockphoto, 17 (right); © Daniel Stein/iStockphoto, 5; © Cassie Tait/iStockphoto, 10; NREL/DOE, photo by Jim Green,
18; Photolibrary © Paul Andrew Lawrence/Alamy, 13; Photolibrary © Ian Middleton/Alamy, 21; Photolibrary/Blend/David Buffington,
4 (left); Rob Cruse Photography, 28; © Noam Armonn/Shutterstock, 11; © Mircea Bezergheanu/Shutterstock, 25, 30 (left); © Adrian
Grosu/Shutterstock, 4 (right); © MaleWitch/Shutterstock, 24; © Greg Randles/Shutterstock, 16; © runamock/Shutterstock, 20; ©
Darryl Sleath/Shutterstock, 27; © Kamil Sobócki/Shutterstock, 17; © Ian Stewart/Shutterstock, 6; © Solar Sailor Holdings Ltd, 23.

135642

Contents

Glossary Words

When a word is printed in **bold**, you can look up its meaning in the Glossary on page 31.

What Is Energy?

Energy makes things work. Many machines need electrical energy to work. The more machines we use, the more electrical energy, or **electricity**, we need. Electrical energy is made in power stations.

electric karaoke machine

DVD player

These machines use electricity from a power station.

Most of the energy we use is made by burning **fossil fuels**, such as coal. Fossil fuels are running out because we use them too much. We need to use other sources to make **alternative energy**.

Burning fossil fuels releases pollution into the air.

Renewable Energy

Energy sources that will not run out are called renewable sources. Energy sources that will run out are called nonrenewable sources. Fossil fuels are a nonrenewable energy source.

The wind is a renewable energy source.

Sustainable Energy

Sustainable energy is made from renewable energy sources. These sources will still be available in the future. They will not run out.

Comparing Energy Sources		
Energy Source	Renewable	Sustainable
Solar energy	✔	✔
Wind energy	✔	✔
Water energy	✔	✔
Nuclear energy	✘	✘
Biofuels	✔	✔
Fossil fuels	✘	✘

Wind Energy

Energy from the wind is called wind energy.
Wind cannot be seen but it can be felt.

These people cannot see the wind, but they can feel it blowing against them.

Wind is moving air. The air moves because it has been warmed by the Sun.

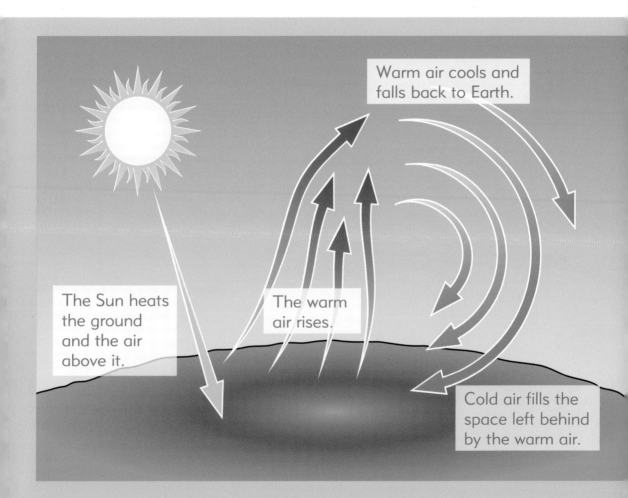

Warm air cools and falls back to Earth.

The Sun heats the ground and the air above it.

The warm air rises.

Cold air fills the space left behind by the warm air.

Wind is the movement of warm and cold air.

Wind Energy in Nature

Natural wind energy:

- scatters plant seeds
- helps birds rest their wings during flight
- blows dead leaves from trees
- pushes clouds across the sky
- makes waves on lakes and seas

This bird uses natural wind energy to glide and rest its wings.

People use natural wind energy to dry their washing. Natural wind energy also moves sail boats along the water and keeps kites flying high in the sky.

Natural wind energy keeps this kite up in the air.

Making Electricity

Wind energy can be changed into electricity using a wind turbine. This electricity is a clean, safe, renewable energy. No fossil fuels are burned to make it.

A wind turbine turns wind energy into electricity we can use.

A wind turbine works if there is enough wind to spin its blades. Wind turbines are useful in **remote** places that are not close to an electricity supply.

These small wind turbines provide electricity for this remote area.

How a Wind Turbine Works

When the wind blows, it spins the blades of the wind turbine. The turbine changes the wind energy into electricity.

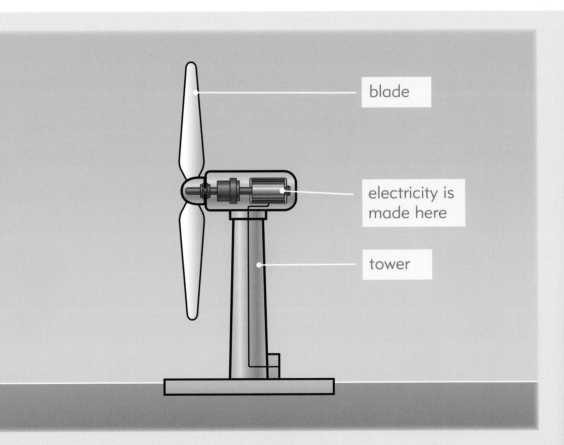

blade

electricity is made here

tower

The electricity created by a wind turbine can be sent through power lines and into buildings.

Most wind turbines sit on tall towers. This allows the turbine blades to catch the strongest winds.

The wind is stronger at the top of the wind turbine.

Some wind turbines look like giant egg beaters.

Wind Farms

Wind farms are places that have a group
of wind turbines used to generate electricity.
More wind turbines can be added when they are

This wind farm has hundreds of wind turbines.

needed. Some wind farms are built **offshore**. The wind turbines sit on the seabed. Because it is very windy at sea, the blades of the wind turbines spin easily.

Offshore wind farms generate a lot of electricity because it is very windy at sea.

Using Wind Energy

Small wind turbines can make enough electricity to provide power to one home.

This small wind turbine provides some of the electricity for this home.

Some people make their own small wind turbines by using recycled items, such as oil drums cut in half.

This wind turbine has been made from recycled materials.

Wind Energy on Farms

Some farmers use wind energy to pump water from underground. Farmers use this water to grow **crops** and to provide drinking water for farm animals.

The wind spins the windmill and this pumps water up from beneath Earth's surface.

A bird-scare device can help stop birds from eating crops. When the wind blows, the device moves and makes a noise. This frightens the birds away.

This bird-scare device moves and makes a noise when the wind blows.

Wind-powered Transportation

Natural wind energy can move things across land and water, and through the air. Wind-powered vehicles are a clean form of transportation.

sail boats

hang glider

Wind-powered vehicles use natural wind energy to move.

Big ships use engines to move through the sea, but some also have special sails. When it is windy out at sea, these ships use their sails instead of their engines.

This ship can run on energy from fossil fuels, the wind, and the Sun.

Wind Energy for Fun

Natural wind energy is also used for activities that are fun, such as windsurfing, wind-skating, and hot-air ballooning.

Sports such as windsurfing do not use fossil fuels and do not pollute the air.

Flying a Kite

Flying a kite is another activity that is fun and uses safe, clean, renewable wind energy. It gives the flyer plenty of exercise and fresh air.

Natural wind energy is used to fly kites and to keep them in the air.

The Future of Wind Energy

Scientists are designing more efficient wind turbines so that more electricity can be made. This means there will be less need to burn fossil fuels for energy.

This wind turbine makes enough electricity for 1,800 homes.

Some wind turbines are combined with solar panels. If the wind is not blowing but the sun is shining, electricity can still be made. This is called a **hybrid energy source**.

A hybrid energy source combines different sources of energy.

Using Less Energy

Using less energy will **conserve** energy sources. People can use less electricity by making sure **appliances** work properly. Appliances that work properly are more **energy-efficient**.

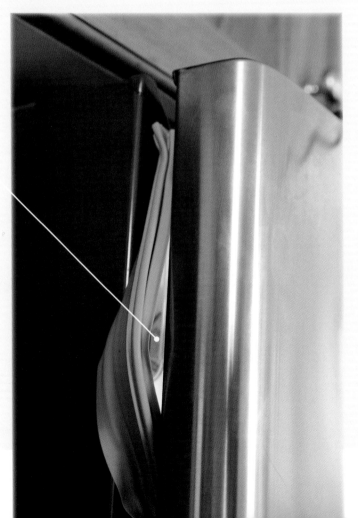

cold air leaks out through this gap

This refrigerator is not energy-efficient because the door cannot close properly.

Another way to be energy-efficient at home is to keep warm air in during winter. Less energy is used for heating if warm air cannot escape.

During winter, close doors and windows to keep warm air in and cold air out.

How Can We Help?

Everybody can help the environment by using less energy. We can use less energy by:

- playing with wind-powered toys
- hanging washing out to dry instead of using the clothes dryer

Wind-powered toys and kites are fun to play with and do not need electricity to work.

Glossary

alternative energy Energy made from a source, such as the wind, instead of from fossil fuels.

appliances Machines, such as refrigerators or televisions, which need electricity to work.

conserve Save.

crops Plants grown for food.

electricity Electrical energy that is carried along a wire.

energy-efficient Uses energy without waste.

fossil fuels Coal, oil, and gas.

hybrid energy source Uses more than one source of energy.

offshore Out at sea.

remote A long way away from cities and difficult to get to.

Index